the
LOVE POEMS
of
RUMI

Brimming with creative inspiration, how-to projects, and useful
information to enrich your everyday life, Quarto Knows is a favorite
destination for those pursuing their interests and passions. Visit our
site and dig deeper with our books into your area of interest:
Quarto Creates, Quarto Cooks, Quarto Homes, Quarto Lives,
Quarto Drives, Quarto Explores, Quarto Gifts, or Quarto Kids.

Inspiring | Educating | Creating | Entertaining

First published in 2015 by Wellfleet Press,
an imprint of The Quarto Group,
142 West 36th Street 4th Floor,
New York, NY 10018, USA
T (212) 779-4972 F (212) 779-6058
www.QuartoKnows.com

Wellfleet Press titles are also available at discount for retail, wholesale, promo-
tional, and bulk purchase. For details, contact the Special Sales Manager by email
at specialsales@quarto.com or by mail at The Quarto Group, Attn: Special Sales
Manager, 401 Second Avenue North, Suite 310, Minneapolis, MN 55401, USA.

10 9 8 7 6

ISBN-13: 978-1-57715-118-0

Design by Erin Fahringer

Printed in China

the
LOVE POEMS
of
RUMI

TRANSLATED BY NADER KHALILI

WELLFLEET
PRESS

Unknown Existence

unknown existence
undiscovered beauty
that's how you are
so far
but
one dawn
just like a sun
right from within
you will arise

In This Earth

in this earth
in this earth
in this immaculate field
we shall not plant any seeds
except for compassion
except for love

All The Precious Words

all the precious words
you and i have exchanged
have found their way
into the heart of the universe
one day they'll pour on us
like whispering rain
helping us arise
from our roots again

The Sweetheart

the sweetheart
who is blocking my sleep
demands tears on my knees
throwing me silently
into the waves
changing the water
to liquid sweet

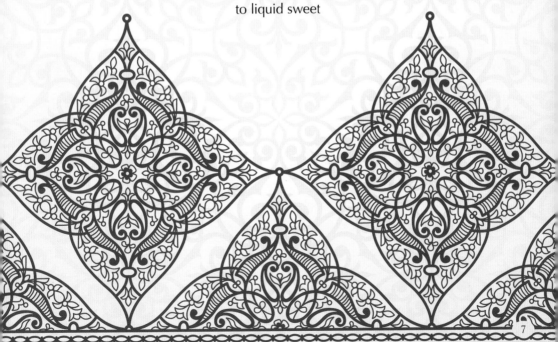

I Know of a Path in Your Heart

i know of a path in your heart
that merges with mine
my sweetheart
i know of a tranquil sea
within me
that mirrors your moon-face
with delight

I Shall Talk to You

i shall talk to you
with no words
i shall whisper to you
no ears will hear
even if among the crowd
i tell my story
i know my tales
can only nest in your ears

My Sweetheart

my sweetheart
the idol of ecstasy
sat by my side
filled with nirvana
embracing the
silken string harp
playing the tune
"i am happy
and i am here
without me"

It's High Time

it's high time
to be only thinking of you
heating your body
with flame and glow
you are a gold mine
hidden in the earth
to purify you
we must set you
on fire

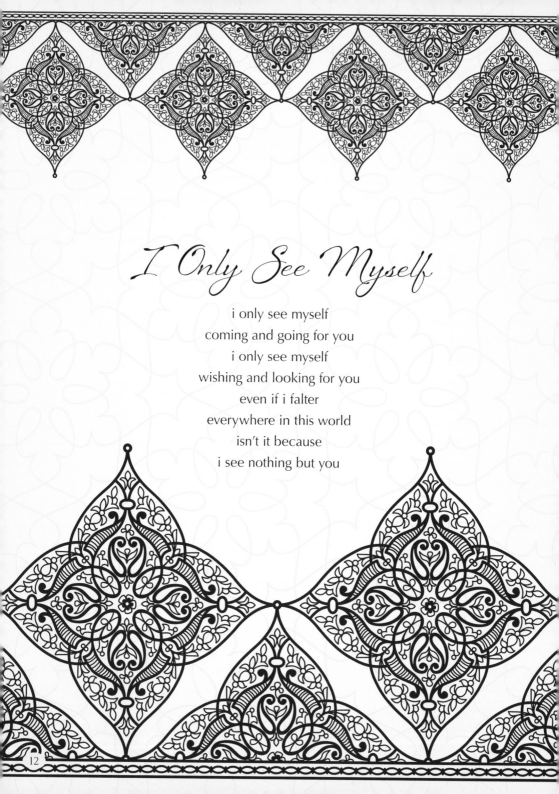

I Only See Myself

i only see myself
coming and going for you
i only see myself
wishing and looking for you
even if i falter
everywhere in this world
isn't it because
i see nothing but you

The Sweetheart in My Dream

the sweetheart in my dream
last night
had the soul and body
of a silver sea
asking everyone
today as i seek
hoping again to find
longing again to see

If You Want To Be Happy

if you want to be happy
and dwell with me
let go of your
double heartedness and be
then you'll become
you with me as you were
and i'll become
me with you as i was

You Are The Letter

you are the letter
written by God
you are the mirror
that reflects the divine
seek inside for
all you want is all you are
there is nothing
above and beyond

Your Soul and Mine

your soul and mine
were one at the roots
our in and out
were one at the heart
i am naive
calling that yours or mine
since me and you
has vanished
from
you and i

This Love is The Owner

this love is the owner
of my bread cloth and home
this love has taken
my body eyes and soul
there is one more thing
it's taken away from me
i can't tell
till there is
the right group
place and time

Take Me In My Love

take me in my love
take my soul
set me on ecstasy
take both of my worlds
if i rest my heart on
anything but you
throw me with fireball
take everything i hold

Wake Up

wake up
let's run wild
in the moonlight
wake up
let's interrupt
the sleep of narcissus
we've been sailing on ice
for a long time
it's high time to
venture the waves now

All I've Asked From You

all i've asked from you
is you and you again
from your love
i've already spread our feast
i don't remember
what i dreamt last night
all i know is
i woke up drunk

I Was In Rage

i was in rage
love said be quiet
i kept silence
love said have you no rage
i was on fire
love said go tranquil
i went tranquil
love said have you no fire

I Can't Let You Know

i can't let you know
all the secrets
i can't open to you
all the doors
there is something inside
that makes me happy
but i can't put my finger
on its source

Come My Love

come my love
you're the precious sun
without you
living colors
in leaves and gardens
are gone
without you it's all
dust and dark
come my love
my party has no spark

Sweetheart I See Myself

sweetheart i see myself
very close to you
like earth
i welcome your every step
is it fair to call you
my entire world
and yet not
find you around

I Came to This World

i came to this world
riding a horse named love
every night is bright
with ecstasy and delight
since in my religion
the intoxication by
pure wine is allowed
you will never see
my lips gone dried

It's Your Voice

it's your voice
making me sing so fine
hearing your call
and I'm generous like God
you've owned me
a hundred times
buy me once more
give me a new life

Those Eyes of Yours

those eyes of yours
teach me divine laws
that love of yours
makes my soul spark
if i'm safe
from evil eyes
it's only because
i'm blessed
by your eyes

Love and Love Alone

love and love alone
that's all I've known
in the beginning, the middle
and to the end unknown
someone is calling me
i think it's my soul
open the door
lazy in love
answer the call

My Dear Heart

my dear heart
hope is all you have
don't let it go
if the entire world
is up against you
hold onto your pal
there are wondrous
secrets going on

God Will Renew Your Life

God will renew your life
when this one is done
your essence remains
when the perishable is gone
love is
the water of life
step inside
every drop
of this sea
holds the promise
of a different life

When I Die

when i die
hand me over
to my sweetheart
one kiss
on my dead lips
don't be surprised
if i come alive

There Was a Time

there was a time
when my thought
soared as a king
or a time when i mourned
like a prisoner
those days are gone
and i have promised
not to take myself
seriously again

I Don't Really Need Wine

i don't really need wine
to get drunk
i don't really need music
to feel delight
without a wine pal
music and dance
i'm intoxicated
happy and gone

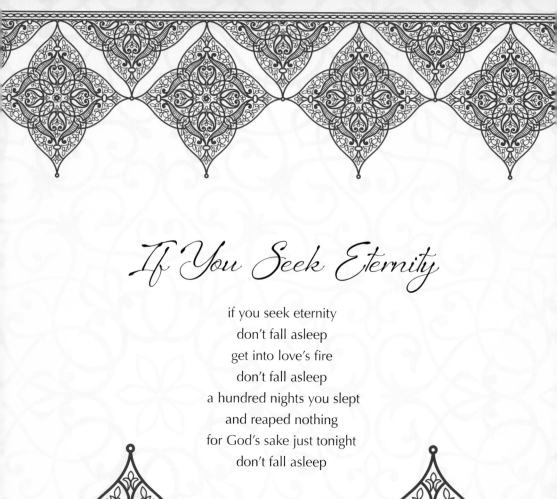

If You Seek Eternity

if you seek eternity
don't fall asleep
get into love's fire
don't fall asleep
a hundred nights you slept
and reaped nothing
for God's sake just tonight
don't fall asleep

Loving My Beloved

loving my beloved
i'm happy tonight
leaving my worries alone
i'm free tonight
dancing and praying
oh God
let the key to the dawn
be lost tonight

Dawn Again and Morning

dawn again and morning
is unleashing someone's love
in a magic aroma
enough sleep the world is leaving
take a deep breath
or the caravan
will take away your share

You've Finally Filled The World With Happiness

you've finally filled the
world with happiness
the earth and the sky
are thrilled
no one is complaining
any more except
the unhappiness
since you broke
everyone free
from its chains

Whatever Happened Between You and Me Last Night

whatever happened between
you and me last night
i can neither write
nor say a word
the day i take my last journey
out of this old country
there will be legend
wrapped around my shroud

I Seek Fire

i seek fire
that's my longing for you
i seek a way out
that's how i'm at your door
i'm sick and tired
of being so unhappy
only you can show me
the time of my life

When I First Fell In Love

when I first fell in love
my neighbors couldn't rest for
my long lamenting times
now that my lamenting
has gone down
the real love
begins to surface
as high fire
catches on
smoke disappears

If You're a Seeker

if you're a seeker
find the company
of seekers
if you're in love
sit by the gate
of those in love
when you've experienced it all
then leave the humans alone
take the company
of no one but God

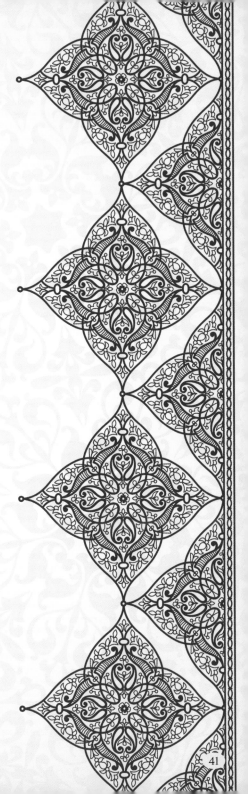

I Am In Love
With Love

i am in love with love
love is in love with me
my body fell in love
with my soul
and my soul fell in love
with me
we take turns in loving
we take turns in being loved

Love Is

love is
a great suspended sea
full of old secrets
full of sinking souls
only a drop
holding a bit of hope
and the rest
nothing but fears

Love Is

love is
what makes people happy
love is
what justifies our being
i was given birth by
the mother
who is called love
to that mother i bestow
a hundred blessings
a hundred cheers

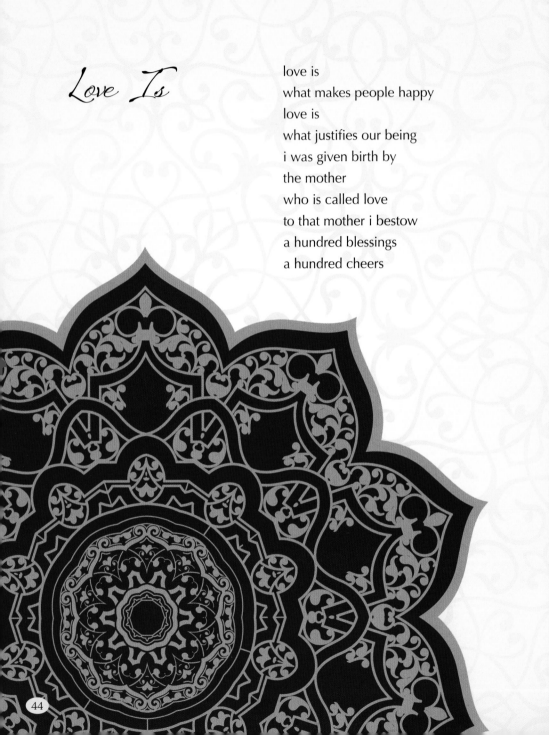

Love Is

love is
best when many
sufferings arise from it
the one who avoids pain
can't know love
a hero is one
who in the journey of love
surrenders his life
with no qualms

Love Is

love is
from the start to eternity
and the seekers of love
are countless forever
and tomorrow
on the day of judgment
any heart who is empty of love
will surely fail to pass

Love Is

love is
the alchemy of the rising sun
a hundred thousand
lightnings in a cloud
and within me
the majesty of love
spreads a sea
drowning all the
galaxies above

Love Is

love is
a mirror
you see nothing
but your reflection
you see nothing
but your real face

I'll Leap Hundred Stages

i'll leap hundred stages
beyond any wisdom
i'll break free
from all known good or bad
i have so much goodness
hidden inside
i'll finally fall in love
with no one but me

Any One In Love

any one in love
must drink day and night
till breaking the evil of
wisdom and shyness
love knows no
body or soul
there is only oneness
and no more

Any One In Love

any one in love
will have no religion
in the religion of love
there is no heresy or faith
love knows no
body heart or soul
there is only
oneness and no more

Your Lover May Seem Timid

your lover may seem timid
what can he do
sleepless
going around your home
what can he do
when he kisses a lock of your hair
don't get mad
if a madman doesn't try
to break the chain
what can he do

All Those In Love Are Ready

all those in love are ready
to lose both worlds
in one stroke
let go of a
hundred years of life
in one day
travel a thousand miles
to experience a moment
and lose a thousand lives
for the sake of one heart

Fallen In Love With You

fallen in love with you
i will take no advice
i have tasted the poison
what good can sugar do
they say he is mad
and in chains
he must be put
mad is my heart
what is a chain
on my foot

In The Journey of Love

in the journey of love
a thousand hearts and souls
will not suffice
only a traveller
ready to give a hundred lives
in every step
and not look back
can take this path

Since
I Have
Learned

since i have learned
to love you
i've closed my eyes
to everyone
every flame
that love strikes
first catches on me
since i've been
scorched before

No Way I'll Let Anyone

no way i'll let anyone
take away this pain
no way i would
lose this love till i die
this gift of pain
given by my beloved
i won't exchange for all
the healing in the world

I Am Ready To Bow

i am ready to bow
to you my beloved
since today i'm more
intoxicated than you are
i'm ready to swear on this
but why swear
if you can't believe me
i'd rather have more wine

I Know The Habits

i know the habits
of my sweetheart
i am the oil and
the beloved's soul is fire
the tenderness of my soul
is from the light
my beloved beams
the darkness around
my sweetheart
is from the smoke
that i spread

I'm So In Love With Your Face

i'm so in love with your face
what do you think i should do
i'm shy to look at
your happy eyes
what do you think i should do
every moment
the pang of love
makes me scream
for God's sake
what do you think i should do

Your Super Perfection

your super perfection
teaches me how to love
i get my love poems and odes
by simply looking at you
my love poems and odes arrive
your dancing image
playing alive
on my heart's stage
that's the source
of my own happy dances

Your Love Is

your love is
in place of religion
and faith for me
as long as i live
i don't want to learn
patience in love
i thought to leave you alone
for a few days
i simply couldn't
why pretend it now

I Have Become

i have become
the owner of a land
with no time and place
i have become the mystic
of a treasure
filled with gold
with a heart burning
in the mother of pearl
i have become
a sea of gracing souls

I'm Your Flute

i'm your flute
i only drink
from your lips
unless you play me
i have no sound
of my own
if you see me silent
i'm treasuring
your sweetness within

I Used To Be Wise and Clever

i used to be wise and clever
just like you
i used to brush aside
all the claims of
the existence of love
now that i'm lost
crazy and carefree
it seems i've been
living this way
all along

The Drum Begs For

the drum begs for
the drummer's beat
with every strike saying
i'll tell a new tale
if you beat me
with mercy or rage
like all lovers
i'll be happy
to tell my tale

Hide My Secrets

hide my secrets
within your soul
keep my world
hidden from your world
if your spirit lets you
wrap my spirit
with yours
make this heresy of mine
the guiding light of yours

Life Without You Is A Waste

life without you is a waste
how can it be named life
if you're not there
i swear a life without you
will not be called anything
but death

If You're Happy

if you're happy
even for a moment
with your sweetheart
seize the moment
as the fulfillment
of your life
beware
let no breath
go to waste
since you will not find
that breath again

You're In My Eyes Otherwise

you're in my eyes otherwise
how could i see
you're in my mind otherwise
how could i be in love
yonder where
i know not where
if your love is not there
how could i be present

This Heart Will One Day

this heart will one day
find you a sweetheart
this soul will one day
take you to the beloved
seize your pain as a blessing
your pain will one day
lead you to healing

You're Like A Flower

you're like a flower
born from the
essence of laughter
good fortune and happiness
you're free and luscious
like a blossoming branch

My Dear Friend

my dear friend
don't expect me
to sustain for you
in grief
don't expect anything
from me but happiness
intoxication and good times
since God created us
only for this
I wreck logic and
fight a sober mind

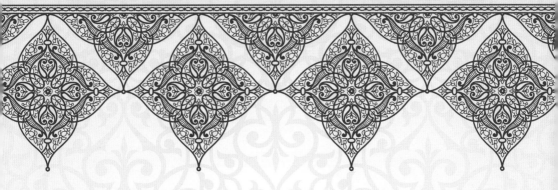

If You Won't Fall in Love

if you won't fall in love
go spin your wool
hundreds of busy works
and changes of color
if your skull is empty
of the wine of love
you might as well
lick the bowl
of those who do

Love Arrived And

love arrived and
like blood
filled my skin and veins
emptied me out and
re-filled with my friend
my beloved has taken over
every part of me
nothing is left of me
but an empty name

If There Is No Fire

if there is no fire
in the heart
then what is this smoke
if it isn't incense burning
then what is this aroma
why me falling in love
and vanishing away
why a candle moth burning
yet happy in flame

For Awhile
Wisdom Came

for awhile wisdom came
to advise the ones
who are in love
it sat by the wayside
to corrupt their way
since it found no room
within their minds
it kissed their feet
and went on its way

Make Your Journey

make your journey
at night
since the night will lead you
to many secrets
and hide you
from your enemies
at night hearts are loving
and eyes sleepy
all night long
we're busy
with no one
but the sweetheart

Anyone Who Is Not In Love

anyone who is not in love
cannot be as light as a soul
like moon and stars
cannot be orbiting restlessly
hear it from me
as the final word
a flag can never dance
with no air and no wind

You're Fulfilled

you're fulfilled
i'm not
so what's the cure
if there's no love
what's the other choice
you said if i show patience
i'll be rewarded with faith
you're the believer of faith
tell me
without the beloved
what is a faith

This Flaring Chest Of Mine

this flaring chest of mine
is filled
with my beloved's teachings
and today that I've fallen ill
is nothing but a fever of love
i'll be glad to avoid
anything my doctor orders
except of course
for honey and wine
offered by my beloved's lips

Who Owns All These Wines

who owns all these wines
which have no grail
who set the trap
while we caught the bird
who owns all this
delicious honey
pistachio and almond
and pours it constantly
on every one
who falls in love

In My Heart

in my heart
inside and out
is all beloved
in my body
blood and veins
is none but beloved
how can there be any
room for religion
or Godlessness in me
since my existence
is overflowing
with beloved

Searching For Love

searching for love
once in a while
we feel at a loss
feeling the pain
of separation
once in a while
we sizzle in fire
once you and i
are cleansed from
the you and the me
only then you and i
without this us
will be happy

I Break
All The Rules

i break all the rules
in pains and healings
i break all the rules
in love and sufferings
you saw me repent
many times with pure heart
now watch me break
my repentances all

I Don't Imagine

i don't imagine
even our soul
is as close to us
as the one we love
i swear to God i never
try to remember my beloved
remembering is only
for those who are absent in us

My Dear Heart

my dear heart
you'll never lose
in love
how can you close
your soul while you become
the soul
in the beginning
you descended from
heavens to earth
and at the end
you'll ascend
from the earth to heaven

Rise O Day

rise o day
the particles desire dancing
to the one
the air and the cosmos
are dancing
happy souls
with no head or feet
will be dancing
and i'll whisper
in your ear
where the dance
will take place

O Love

o love
they think of you
as an angel
or as a human
or above and beyond
the Solomon's seal
they think of you
as the soul's dwelling
in the universe's mold
but i live with you
as no one ever knows

This Love Is Heading To

this love is heading to
where the brave are
this bold deer moves
into the lion's den
this house of love
has flourished with
hopes and dreams
do you imagine
it will fall apart
without you

I Was A Pious Preacher

i was a pious preacher
you changed me to a poet
and in me you instilled
rebel rousing and
drunkenness in every feast
i was a solemn
man of sustained prayer
you made me the playing object
of street children

Without Love

without love
partying and good times
won't go very far
without love
human existence
won't elate and evolve
if a hundred drops of rain
fall from the clouds
over the sea
without the motion
of love
not one drop
can create a hidden
precious pearl

Come

come
whoever you are
come
come again
even if you are godless
and a worshipper of
fire and idols
come
our home is the home of
never losing hope
come
even if you break
your repentance vows
a hundred times
come again
come

Come Inside the Fire

come inside the fire
leave your trickery behind
go insane
go mad
burn like a candle-moth

first make yourself a stranger
to yourself and
tear down your house
then move with us
dwell in the abode of love

wash your chest
seven times over
cleansing from hatred
then mold yourself into the chalice
holding the pure wine of love

to understand the intoxicated
you must become intoxicated
to join the eternal soul
you must become a soul

you heard my story and
your spirit grew wings
now you must be annihilated in love
to become a fable of your own

your imagination my friend flies away
then pulls you as a follower
surpass the imagination and
like fate
arrive ahead of yourself

passion and desire
has locked your heart
you must become the key
the teeth of the key
to open all locks

King Solomon gives you a message
listen to the birds
they are talking to you
calling you a trap
frightening them away

to capture us they say
you must make a nest
you must make a nest

your sweetheart's face
is appearing now
change yourself to a mirror
and fill yourself to the brim

so many gifts
you purchased for your love
quit buying gifts
give yourself over

you were a part of the
mineral kingdom in the beginning
then you changed to animal life for awhile
then you found the soul of human for awhile
now the time has arrived
to become
the soul of the souls

I Am No Lion

i am no lion
to overpower my enemies
winning over myself
if i can
is enough

though i'm of lowly earth
since i nourish a seed
named love
i'll grow
lilies of the field

when i'm pitch-black
lamenting separation
i know for sure
i will break through
spreading light on the dark night

i am on fire inside
but look grim outside
since i want to rise
like smoke through my cell

i am a child
whose teacher is love
surely master
won't let me grow
to be a fool

I've Come Again

i've come again
like a new year
to crash the gate
of this old prison

i've come again
to break the teeth and claws
of this man-eating
monster we call life

i've come again
to puncture the
glory of the cosmos
who mercilessly
destroys humans

i am the falcon
hunting down the birds
of black omen
before their flights

i gave my word
at the outset to
give my life
with no qualms

i pray to the Lord
to break my back
before i break my word

how do you dare to
let someone like me
intoxicated with love
enter your house

you must know better
if i enter
i'll break all this and
destroy all that

if the sheriff arrives
i'll throw the wine
in his face
if your gatekeeper
pulls my hand
i'll break his arm

if the heavens don't go round
to my heart's desire
i'll crush its wheels and
pull out its roots

you have set up
a colorful table
calling it life and
asked me to your feast
but punish me if
i enjoy myself

what tyranny is this

Restless

restless
now i go to the door
now i go on the roof
till i see your face
i'll never know rest

neighbors speak of me
when you are away
as meek or mad
but when you return
everything subsides

this heart of mine
tears itself apart
and seeks no joy
but only wants to know
when you'll arrive

but when you return
and a wine-server is around
i hold a cup
fondle your hair and
caress your face

just come and see me
letting go of my wish
letting go of my pilgrimage
keeping one wish in my heart
making love to your desires

Rocks Crack Apart

rocks crack apart
filled with passions
longing to have
a glimpse of you

soul grows wings
over-joyed with desire
flying in search of you

fire changes to water
wisdom becomes insanity
and my own eyes
turn out to be the enemy
of my sleep
as they long to see you

there is a dragon
devouring rocks and men
causing insanity
destroying peaceful lives
and calling itself love

please
don't imprison free souls
don't change laughter to cries
don't press us so hard
there is no one
but you to turn to

your love demands
nothing less than
my wounded heart
and my heart is filled
with nothing but your longings

the wine jar is boiling over
someone is drinking the wine
and making the harp play itself
the sonnets to your admiration

your love entered my house
saw me without you
put its hand over my head
and said pity on you

this love journey
is surely the hardest and
most twisted road I have taken
i began the journey but my heart
is still dragging behind
wrapped around your feet

How Very Close

how very close
is your soul with mine
i know for sure
everything you think
goes through my mind

i am with you
now and doomsday
not like a host
caring for you
at a feast alone

with you i am happy
all the times
the time i offer my life
or the time
you gift me your love

offering my life
is a profitable venture
each life i give
you pay in turn
a hundred lives again

in this house
there are a thousand
dead and still souls
making you stay
as this will be yours

a handful of earth
cries aloud
i used to be hair or
i used to be bones

and just the moment
when you are all confused
leaps forth a voice
hold me close
i'm love and
i'm always yours

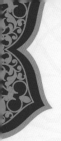

Only You

only you
i choose
among the entire world

is it fair
of you
letting me be unhappy

my heart
is a pen
in your hand

it is all
up to you
to write me happy or sad

i see only
what you reveal
and live as you say

all my feelings
have the color
you desire to paint

from the beginning
to the end
no one but you

please make
my future
better than the past

when you hide
i change
to a Godless person

and when you
appear
i find my faith

don't expect
to find any more in me
than what you give

don't search for
hidden pockets because
i've shown you that
all i have
is all you gave

I Am

i am
the minstrel of
eternal love
and will play
the song of happiness

when my soul
hears music
and changes to softness
i'll break open
the wine jar's seal

i am in love
with the temple of fire
because i was born
as the prophet
named Khalili Abraham

i am in love
with soul and
wisdom
i am the enemy
of false images

the spring is arriving
it is high time
for action
for the sun and Aries
to get together

my blood is boiling
my heart is on fire and
the winter snow
is melting away
from my body

someone's love
is knocking me out
and pulling me
after itself
very forcefully

though i am
in this
hell and fire
i'm filled with
honey and nectar

though i am
condemned to take
this journey
i'm filled with
the sweetness of going home

now the time has come
my sweetheart
kindly express
what my tongue
can never describe

You Ask Me

you ask me
who are you and
with such a shaky
existence how can you
fall in love

how do i know
who am i or where i am
how could a single wave
locate itself
in an ocean

you ask me
what am i seeking
above and beyond
the pure light
that i once was

and why am i
imprisoned in this cage
named body and
yet i claim to be
a free bird

how do i know
how i lost my way
i know for sure
i was all straight
before i was
seduced by love

Come

come
let's fall
in love
again

let's run
all the dirt
in this world
to shiny gold

come
let's be
a new spring
a love re-born

find our aroma
from the essence
of all who
emit heavenly fragrance

like a fresh tree
bloom and spread
all the blessings
right from inside

How Long

how long
can i see myself
chained in this prison
chained in this world

the time has come
to take my good life
in my hands and
gallop to the sublime

finally purified
i'm no more polluted
and from now on
i'll take my quests
directly to God Himself

i was given
at my birth
all the estates and mansions
it will be a heresy
to accept only
a doorkeeper's job

now my dear heart
since you and i are all alone
having your midnight message
i'll do exactly
that which you know

once i alter this
doorkeeper's attitude
once i change the
essence in my mind
happiness will replace misery

once i grow wings
in place of my slow feet
all obstacles will vanish
and i really can fly in
time and space again

I Was Dead

I was dead
i came alive
i was tears
i became laughter

all because of love
when it arrived
my temporal life
from then on
changed to eternal

love said to me
you are not
crazy enough
you don't
fit this house

i went and
became crazy
crazy enough
to be in chains

love said you are not
intoxicated enough
you don't
fit the group

i went and
got drunk
drunk enough
to overflow
with light – headedness

love said
you are still
too clever
filled with
imagination and skepticism

i went and
became gullible
and in fright
pulled away
from it all

love said
you are a candle
attracting everyone
gathering everyone
around you

i am no more
a candle spreading light
i gather no more crowds
and like smoke
i am all scattered now

love said
you are a teacher
you are a head
and for everyone
you are a leader

i am no more
not a teacher
not a leader
just a servant
to your wishes

love said
you already have
your own wings
i will not give you
more feathers

and then my heart
pulled itself apart
and filled to the brim
with a new light
overflowed with fresh life

now even the heavens
are thankful that
because of love
i have become
the giver of light

All My Friends

all my friends
departed like dreams
left alone
i called upon
one friend
to become
my entire dream

this is the one
who soothes my heart
with endless
tenderness and love

the one who
one hour bestows
inner peace
and the next
the nectar of life

this dream too
as it arrives
i come alive and as it departs
i'm helpless again

Believe Me

believe me
i wasn't always like this
lacking common sense
or looking insane

like you
i used to be clever
in my days

never like this
totally enraptured
totally gone

like sharp shooters
i used to be
a hunter of hearts

not like today
with my own heart
drowning in its blood

nonstop asking and
searching for answers
that was then

but now
so deeply enchanted
so deeply enthralled

always pushing
to be ahead and above
since i was not yet hunted down
by this
ever-increasing love

Whenever You Meet

whenever you meet
someone deep drunk
yet full of wisdom
be aware and watch
this person is enthralled
only by love

anytime you see
someone who seems gone
tipsy and happy
filled with rapture
be sure and observe
this is the condition
of someone in love

if you see a head
happy and thrilled
filled with joy
every night and day
this head was fondled
by the fingers of love

every moment
someone is blessed
a tree sprouts
an angel flies
even a monster
leaps with delight

when your body
feels together
when your soul
wants to unite
you are chosen
for a blissful of love

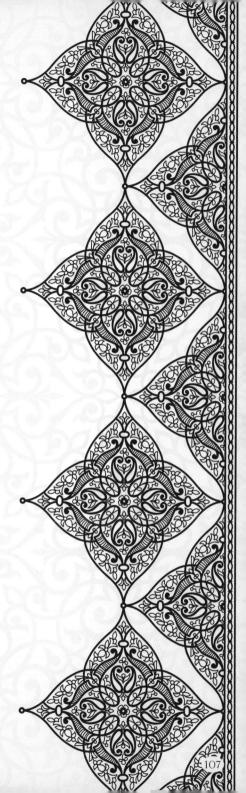

Rebellious I Feel Again

rebellious i feel again
i swear i can tear
every chain
you wrap around me

i'm that crazy
fastened fellow who
cages monsters
by his magical tongue

i don't want
this mortal life
i don't desire
this mortal soul

you my life
you my soul
you my love
that's who i want

when you hide away
i feel darkness in my faith
and when you appear
i'm filled with grace

if i drank from this jar
it's because of your reflection
and if i breathe without you
i regret it for the rest of my life

without you i swear
even if i fly
i'm sad
as a dark cloud

without you
even in a rose garden
i fell in prison
i swear again

the music in my ear
is only your name
the dance of my soul
is only with your wine

please come again
and reconstruct
this house of mine
this is my existence

going to an abbey
or going to a mosque
i'm only there
in search of you

Running And Leaping Nonstop

running and leaping nonstop
till I catch up
with the fastest rider

annihilating forever
vanishing for good
till I reach the soul of the world

very happy I've become
ever since I changed
to a piece of fire

and with this fire
I'll burn my house and
dwell in the desert

i'll soften and humble
i'll change the earth
till i grow your flowers in me

i'll crawl and flow
i'll change myself to water
till i can reach your paradise garden

without pain no healer
will tend me
or give me potions

i'll change to
total pain
till i get total healing

ever since i was born
i was thrown into this world
helpless and shivering
like a speck of dust in the air

but as soon as i reach
the end of this journey
and settle down
i'll be secure and tranquil forever

I've Come To Take You

i've come to take you
with me
even if i must drag you along
but first must steal your heart
then settle you in my soul

i've come as a spring
to lay beside your blossoms
to feel the glory of happiness
and spread your flowers around

i've come to show you off
as the adornment of my house
and elevate you to the heavens
as the prayers of those in love

i've come to take back
the kiss you once stole
either return it with grace
or i must take it by force

you're my life
you're my soul
please be my last prayer
my heart must hold you forever

from the lowly earth
to the high human soul
there are a lot more
than a thousand stages

since i've taken you along
from town to town
no way will i abandon
you halfway down this road

though you're in my hands
though i can throw you around
like a child and a ball
i'll always need to chase after you

Once Again

once again
my sweetheart
found me in town

i was hiding from
love's rapture
i was escaping from the tavern
but soon i was found

what's the use of running
no soul can escape
no use hiding
i've found a hundred times

i thought i could hide
in a crowded city
how can i when i was found
among my own crowded secrets

now i celebrate with joy
now i'm happy with my luck
just because no matter how
hard i hide i am found

how can i hide
when all over are the marks
spotting the path of
my bleeding hunted heart

and finally my beloved
handed me as i was found
the cup of wine that washes away
all the worries and unhappiness of
the world

In Every Breath

in every breath
if you're the center
of your own thoughts
the sadness of autumn
will fall on you

but if in every breath
you strip naked
just like a winter
the joy of spring
will grow from within

all your impatience
comes from the push
for gain of patience
let go of the effort
and peace will arrive

all your unfulfilled desires
are from your greed
for gain of fulfillments
let go of them all
and they will be sent as gifts

fall in love with
the agony of love
not the ecstasy
then the beloved
will fall in love with you

If Your Beloved

if your beloved
has the life of a fire
step in now and burn along

in a night full of
suffering and darkness
be a candle spreading light till dawn

stop this useless
argument and disharmony
show your sweetness and accord

even if you fell
torn to pieces
sew yourself new clothes

your body and soul
will surely feel the joy
when you simply go along

learn this lesson from
lute tambourine and trumpet
learn the harmony of the musicians

if one is playing a wrong note
even among twenty
others will stay out of tune

don't say what is the use
of me alone being peaceful
when everyone is fighting

you're not one
you're a thousand
just light your lantern

since one live flame
is better than
a thousand dead souls

Rocking And Rolling

rocking and rolling
what have you been drinking
please let me know

you must be drunk
going house to house
wandering from street to street

who have you been with
who have you kissed
whose face have you been fondling

you are my soul
you are my life
i swear my life and love is yours

so tell me the truth
where is that fountainhead
the one you've been drinking from

don't hide this secret
lead me to the source
fill my jug over and over again

last night i finally caught
your attention in the crowd
it was your image filling my dream

telling me to stop this wandering
stop this search for
good and evil

i said my dear prophet
give me some of
that you've drunk for ecstasy of life

if i let you drink you said
any of this burning flame
it will scorch your mouth and throat

your portion has been
given already by heaven
ask for more at your peril

i lamented and begged
i desire much more
please show me the source

i have no fear
to burn my mouth and throat
i'm ready to drink every flame and more

If You Dwell Very Long

if you dwell very long
in a heart depressed and dark
be aware you've fallen low
in will and quest

a heart filled with grief
whirling and spinning endlessly
can never feel at peace

what makes you
tremble in fear
that's your true worth now

whatever seems to be
your healing source
is the cause of your pain

whatever you think
is sure secure and forever
is what has hunted you down

whenever your mind flies
it can only land
in the house of madness

whenever love arrives
there is no space
for your self claim

a heart filled with love
is like a phoenix
that no cage can imprison

such a bird can only fly
above and beyond
any known universe

Come Let's Speak

come let's speak
of our souls
let's even hide from
our ears and eyes

like a rose garden
always keep a smile
like imagination
talk without a sound

like the spirit
reigning the world
telling the secrets
uttering no word

let's get away from
all the clever humans
who put words in our mouth
let's only say what our hearts desire

even our hands and feet
sense every inner move
let's keep silence
but make our hearts move

the mystery of destiny
know the life of
speck after speck of dust
let's tell our story
as a particle of dust

Your Sudden Journey

your sudden journey
from our city
my beloved
filled you with sweetness
and left me in the dark

you went along
with your own sweetheart
the one for whom
every soul is ready
to leave the body and fly

it was that spectrum
the one who came
first as a light
brightened your path
then took you away in limelight

you were ready
happy to leave this lowly earth
while filled with ecstasy
you flew away with rapture
to the ultimate and beyond

now that you're gone
you've forever found
the ultimate paradise
free from bread
free from bread givers

now you are
like a pure soul
like a dream
every moment
taking a new form

send me some words
of your tender journey
my beloved and
if you don't
i know for sure
you're forever immersed
like a precious pearl
in the endless sea

I'm Not Going To Leave

i'm not going to leave
this house and set out
on a journey any more
i've everything right here

in every corner
a garden of memories
devoid of darkness
devoid of fear

the news of my journey
spreading in this town
is but a rumor of every enemy

how can i think
of going very far
how can i walk headless
how can i go with no soul

how can i ever find
anywhere in this world
a more beautiful face
a more desired beloved

even the moon
is seeking for this love
to see its reflection
to find its adornment

if i ever talk about
going to travel
or leaving this town
break my teeth with no qualms

i've lost my feet
going to the sea of love
but like a boat
i need no feet to crawl

and even if you
throw me out of your door
i'll come back
through the roof hole

because of your love
i'll be dancing and floating
in this air as a speck of dust
to finally settle into your house

Come Down My Love

come down my love
abandon your adventurous flight
it's high time for a happy life

come into my house
throw out my old belongings
burn me again with your love

i know for sure
even if you burn the entire house
your love will build me a new paradise

you empowered the drops of water
to shine like diamonds
you blew life into a piece of clay

you gave a lowly fly
the same wings as an eagle
the aspiration of the sky

there was a blind sage in our town
a healer took mercy on him with medicine
to set his eyes open to the light

the sage refused and replied
if you could only see the light i see
you'd pluck out both of your eyes

My Secret Beloved

my secret beloved
sent me a secret message

"give me your soul
give me your life

wander like a drifter
go on a journey

walk into this fire with grace
be like a salamander

come into your source of flame
fire transmutes to a rose garden

don't you know that my thorn
is better than the queen of roses
don't you know my heresy
is the essence of spirituality

then surrender your spirit
surrender your life"

oh God i know
a garden is better than a cage

i know a palace
is better than a ruin

but i'm that owl in this world
who loves to live in the ruins of love

i may be that poor wandering soul
but watch all the aspiration and light

watch the glow of God
reflecting my face

Look at Love

look at love
how it tangles
with one fallen in love

look at spirit
how it fuses with earth
giving it new life

why are you so busy
with this or that or good or bad
pay attention to how things blend

why talk about all
the known and the unknown
see how unknown merges into the known

why think separately
of this life and the next
when one is born from the last

look at your heart and tongue
one feels but deaf and dumb
the other speaks in words and signs

look at water and fire
earth and wind
enemies and friends all at once

the wolf and the lamb
the lion and the deer
far away yet together

look at the unity of this
spring and winter
manifested in the equinox

you too must mingle my friends
since the earth and the sky
are mingled just for you and me

be like sugarcane
sweet yet silent
don't get mixed up with bitter words

my beloved grows
right out of my own heart
how much more union can there be

My Dear Heart

my dear heart
you're a fire worshiper
an explosive in flame

call on the cupbearer
to sprinkle wind on you
to soothe your burn with water

that special cupbearer
the same one who sizzles
lives with wine and lips with kisses

the one who first calmed my mind
gave me a cup of fiery wine
and took me to a secret house

in that special house
dwelled a precious sweetheart
who offered me a choice

a tray full of gold
a tray full of flame
a few words I was told

this gold is soaked with fire
this fire is filled with gold
if you choose fire you'll end up with gold

if you choose the burden of gold
you'll lay heavy and cold
take the fire of the beloved and leap with joy

I'm Loyal

to the image and beauty
of my beloved
please speak of that image only
and say no more

whenever you are with me
speak only about
the generosity of candles
the generosity of the sugarcane
and say no more

don't speak of any suffering
show me the treasure that waits
at the end of the road
if you're ignorant of the path
then say no more

last night I was in flame
my beloved saw me and said
"I'm here at last
don't tear your clothes
lament no more"

i begged my beloved
to understand my condition
to sense my fear
my love said "when i'm present
you must seek no more

i'll whisper the words
of secrets into your ears
and you must promise not to answer
just nod your head
and say no more

the face of a sweetheart
has penetrated your heart
the tenderness is all there is
your journey is the journey of love
sense it to the depth and say no more"

i asked if the face
belongs to a human
of that of an angel
"neither this nor that
sense it but say no more"

i said if you don't
identify this for me at once
my life will be shattered
"be shattered at once
but say no more

you're dwelling in
a house filled with
images and dreams
pack all your belongings
move out but say no more"

you're simply expressing
the experience of God
i said to the beloved
"yes this is the answer
but for God's sake say no more"

Don't Tell Me I Had Enough

don't tell me i had enough
don't stop me from having more
my soul isn't yet satisfied

last night an intoxicated friend
handed me his wine jar
i broke the jar in spite of my desire

i'm not enslaved
by my craving body
i'll not pollute this endless longing

i've broken the barriers
of the past and future
without being drunk

love's message came to me this morning
hiding itself as a healer
taking my pulse and declaring i'm weak

don't drink wine
given by anyone
but your beloved"

if i can only find i said
the fountainhead named love
what use is any wine

My Dear Friend

my dear friend
never lose hope
when the beloved
sends you away

if you're abandoned
if you're left hopeless
tomorrow for sure
you'll be called again

if the door is shut
right in your face
keep waiting with patience
don't leave right away

seeing your patience
your love will soon
summon you with grace
rise you like a champion

and if all the roads
end up in dead ends
you'll be shown the secret paths
no one will comprehend

the beloved i know
will give with no qualms
to a puny ant
the Kingdom of Solomon

my heart has journeyed
many times around the world
but has never found
and will never find
such a beloved again

ah i better keep silence
i know this endless love
will surely arrive
for you and you and you

If You Can't Go To Sleep

if you can't go to sleep
my dear soul
for tonight
what do you think will happen

if you pass your night
and merge it with dawn
for the sake of heart
what do you think will happen

if the entire world
is covered with blossoms
you have labored to plant
what do you think will happen

if the elixir of life
that has been hidden in the dark
fills the desert and towns
what do you think will happen

if because of
your generosity and love
a few humans find their lives
what do you think will happen

if you pour an entire jar
filled with joyous wine
on the head of those already drunk
what do you think will happen

go my friend
bestow your love
even on your enemies
if you touch their hearts
what do you think will happen

Come Come Come

come come come
my endless desires
come come come

come my beloved
come my sweetheart
come come come

don't talk about the journey
say no more
of the path one must take

you are my path
you are my journey
come come come

you stole from this earth
a bouquet of roses
i am hidden in that bouquet
come come come

as long as i am sober
and keep talking about
good and bad
i'm missing
the most important event
seeing your face
come come come

i must be a moron
missing this life
if i don't cast my mind
in the fire of your love
come come come

About the Translator

Nader Khalili (1936-2008) was a world-renowned Iranian-American architect, author, humanitarian and teacher. Khalili was also the founder and director of the California Institute of Earth Art and Architecture (Cal-Earth).

Khalili was raised by the poetry of Rumi. As a child, his grandmother would recite Rumi's poetry to lull him to sleep. He later developed a passion for studying and translating Rumi's works. Rumi's poetry also became an intrinsic part of Khalili's architectural career. Inspired by the mystical poetry of Rumi, his architecture was distilled from the timeless principles of this universe and its timeless materials—the elements of earth, air, water, and fire, and has been described as "Poetry crystallized into structure."